How I Survived 5 Kidney Transplants And Won!

How I Survived 5 Kidney Transplants and Won!

The Heart Moving Story of a Young Man's Journey to Survive

Darren Ferguson

Darren Ferguson

Copyright Year: April 2017

Copyright Notice: by Darren Ferguson. All rights reserved. No part of this book may be reproduced in any form or by any means whatsoever.

Results in this copyright notice:
© 2017 Darren Ferguson. All rights reserved

ISBN – 978-1-909389-20-5

Dedication

This book is dedicated to all those people who are terrified, scared, depressed and uncertain, when faced with life's challenges; like me, you too, can overcome.

Darren Ferguson

How I Survived 5 Kidney Transplants and Won!

The Heart Moving Story of a Young Man's Journey to Survive

Contents

Acknowledgements	7
Introduction	10
Chapter 1 – It Began At Birth	17
Chapter 2 – Why Was I Different?	21
Chapter 3 – Great Ormond Street	26
Chapter 4 - Transition	32
Chapter 5 – Bad and Good News	37
Chapter 6 – The Struggle Is Real	43
Chapter 7 – Being Thankful	53
Chapter 8 – Finding The 'One'!	59
Chapter 9 – The News	71
The Life of Darren Ferguson	88
AMANDA FERGUSON - WIFE	88
DAD	91
THE THOUGHTS OF A MOTHER	95
SACHEL GRANT	103
LEE FERGUSON	106
CHARMAINE	108
BETHANE CHARLES – NURSE	110

**KIDNEY DISEASE IS A SILENT KILLER: Learn About
This Deadly Disease**   **114**
    WHAT ARE THE KIDNEYS?   114
    TREATMENTS FOR CHRONIC KIDNEY DISEASE   118
    LIFE ON DIALYSIS   120
    KIDNEY TRANSPLANTS   121

About The Author: Darren Ferguson   **124**

Acknowledgements

First and foremost, I must acknowledge Jesus Christ since without him I wouldn't be here to even tell you my story. At different stages in my life, my faith in him was shaken and I was not always the best Christian I could've been but he never gave up on me. Always making a way when others would've given up, he carried me through some of the darkest and challenging times of my life and without him I'm and have nothing and yet, he continues to guide and be with me.

My Parents and Brother, I thank you for your support and words of encouragement when I needed it during the process. I love you all very dearly.

My beautiful wife and children who've put up with me while I wrote this book, the late nights, the times I've been away from home so that I could achieve this dream of mine, thank you... we've done it!

Kwame M.A McPherson thank you for believing in my story and making me live out one of my dreams by writing this book. The times when I'd no motivation, you pushed me to get it completed. Thank you for making it possible.

Paul Harrison from PK Media and Zierlich Dialysis for the opportunity to speak about my journey at the Jamaican High Commission at the Zierlich launch back in 2017.

Great Ormond Street, Royal Free Hospital and the MK Renal Unit, words fail on how to express my gratitude to you all, it has been a journey of tears and laughter, watching me grow from a rebellious boy to an adult man. The many times you could've given up on me too but you persisted with making me better and for that I thank you - this book is for you.

My extended family and close friends who've been there throughout the years and who've seen me at my worst, carried me when I couldn't carry myself, prayed for and with me, had a special word of encouragement and strong support, thank you, from my heart. Thank you.

My Faith Dimensions family, my local church in Milton Keynes, your prayers have seen me through, your warm hearts and open arms were always there any time I was sick and I'm grateful to you. FDM forever!

How I Survived 5 Kidney Transplants and Won!

A very dear person, my Best friend and Brother Tim Ukachi-Lois who sadly passed away in September 2016, Bro today I'm sad because from day one you were there, you always believed in me, you pushed me to be better and to pursue my dream... Bro this is for you, I'm just sorry you're not here to see the finished product but Bro every day I think of your words of wisdom that you gave me during the entire process.

Darren Ferguson

Introduction

Everyone talks about the success of kidney transplants. Rarely do we ever talk about what happens when a transplant fails, the hardships a patient goes through to get back onto the transplant list and receive another transplant if possible, is stressful and frustrating.

As a transplant patient I think it is important to say that we have no control over most causes of transplant failure but we do have control over how we take our medicine and staying as healthy as possible. In general, most transplant patients do take good care of their kidneys as we understand how important it is, though sometimes it can fail on us.

There are a lot of reactions people have whenever their transplanted kidney fails and every situation is different, thus impossible to determine what is a "usual" response. When the transplanted kidney stops working, often, the most common responses are shock and disappointment and we tend to believe it will never happen to us, though we know the risks in having that particular transplant.

How I Survived 5 Kidney Transplants and Won!

For a lot of people, it seems that there is a theme of frustration and sadness when they have to return on dialysis. No matter how long any of my kidneys have worked, it was always discouraging to be told I would need to return to using the dialysis machine, and find this to be devastating news. Some of the struggles people face when they first learn of kidney disease, are also experienced by people who are returning to dialysis after transplant. They wonder what they may have done wrong and why they needed to go through it again. They sometimes consider not returning to dialysis and are angry and sad all the time. Some people are even not ready to deal with the reality of having to return to using dialysis.

We do not know what life is going to throw at any one time and little did I know I would suffer from kidney failure for so many years but also, somehow, go through five kidney transplants was something I never thought I would ever have to deal with.

When I had my first kidney transplant I thought that would be it and I would be able to get on with my life but unfortunately, as with life, we never know what next will happen. One of the hardest things for any kidney patient is having to deal with the rejection once the kidney stops working. It brings your life to an automatic and grinding halt, and all plans cease as mine did in an instant as I returned to be on dialysis for a period of time.

When my body rejected the first kidney, I was still quite young so as upsetting as it was I knew I would get another opportunity and so made sure I stayed reasonably fit, just to be ready.

My second transplant seemed to come around fairly quickly although a few years had passed and maybe I was enjoying life too much, pushing the thought from my mind. Although I do not remember too much about the process, I do remember the day after my transplant I was out of my bed and playing games with the other patients. At that moment, I felt happy I had a working kidney and was able to be a normal child.

As a renal patient you value each day knowing each one could be your last with a working kidney. It is a long journey that only people who have been through it, truly understand. At each hospital appointment, you pray for the good news that everything is well but always, in the back of your mind, you know your doctor, at any moment, can tell you: "Unfortunately, the kidney has stopped functioning".

When this happened to me at this time, all I kept thinking about was living a normal life like everybody else. Why was it that I had to take the time off from school and visit the hospital? Questions were in my mind, fortunately, my wonderful support structure was very good as my family and friends were always a tower of strength for me whenever I needed them most.

My third transplant was one of the hardest challenges I had to face.

I remember being so excited, finally I was getting my life back and I will never forget waking up from the surgery and asking my Mother: "Did it work?" The look on her face told me everything I needed to know. There had been a problem. She told me that the new kidney went into rejection hours after been put in me and needed to be removed. I was devastated. To know I was so close but now so far, right back at the beginning, left me in a wreck.

The emotional pain I felt was greater than the physical pain of the surgery.

I refused to hear anything about going back on dialysis or even having another transplant and for a very long time I was in denial. The whole process was mentally, physically and emotionally draining and yet after a while, I had to come to the realisation that something had to be done. Between the third and fourth transplant, the wait was long and in the back of my mind I had given up. I was not getting any phone calls. I was feeling drained and down. Finally, by the time I did get the call I remembered being extremely calm since I did not want to build my hopes and dreams on a "MAYBE". I also knew that from my past experiences, I could end up on a path of another failure. Nonetheless, I was grateful for the FOURTH opportunity, I had been given another lifeline, another chance to rebuild my life...

But...guess what... this kidney lasted two years.

As much as it may sound funny, this one I could understand, I was working for a company and became careless in looking after myself. There are times things happen in life where we have to take responsibility for our actions and for the first time, I had dropped the ball. I took life and the kidney for granted with the things I used to do. I worked hard and had many late nights and stopped doing the right things, thinking

How I Survived 5 Kidney Transplants and Won!

I could get away with it. Due to my own silly games and neglect, I was about to pay the ultimate price, another rejection. Surely this would be my last and a life on dialysis seem inventible. Little did I know that everyday which passed, the kidney was slowly declining.

I remember been so angry at myself for slipping up, allowing this to happen and the consequences I would pay were all on me. My doctor even told me he was not sure if I would ever get another kidney since there were so many antibodies in my blood.

Slowly the years went by and I remember having a conversation with my doctor and him asking me if there was anybody I could ask. To which I just laughed, how do you have a conversation with somebody asking for their kidney.

To me it sounded so ridiculous but fortunately it got to a point in my life where my closest where asking if they could be a donor to me. Even so, each donor kept returning as negative until I met a lovely guy through a mutual friend. Lee Ferrigon had lost his own wife to cancer, said he wanted to help me. During my wait for a new kidney, he had seen how sick I would be and the very challenging times I experienced since most days I was sick and at times fatigued. People did not know but there were days where my mind would return to the time I had lost my previous kidney and how I paid a very heavy price for it. But, then, I vowed, I would NEVER take my body or a kidney transplant for granted, ever again.

So Lee and I started the process of testing for a transplant with each one returning with flying colours. He was a super fit athlete and the day I heard we were going ahead with the transplant a feeling of shock and disbelief came over me. There was also relief because NOW I would have my life back.

Six years later the kidney is working well and I am grateful for each and every day. I am now able to travel and in the six years I have been able to visit some of the most beautiful places such as New York, Paris, Las Vegas, Jamaica pain free, dialysis free and just embracing each day and with it I think of someone who so kindly gave up a piece of them to save me.

This book is a snapshot of some of my most trying experiences....

Darren Ferguson

Chapter 1 – It Began At Birth

My story really began from birth but I failed to identify it until I was about three weeks old.

Though I was too young to know when my first surgery took place, I do remember receiving letters for appointments at Great Ormond Street Hospital, a leading hospital in the world. I'd always get nervous and upset when visiting; nervous because I wasn't sure what to expect and upset since it meant I would not be able to attend school. Sometimes, I remember going to bed and thinking "will I live to see the morning?" since I was in so much pain that my Mother would come in my room, just to see if I was ok. At one stage, even the hospital had told my parents I wouldn't live past 7-years of age. Finally, I learnt I had Chronic Kidney Failure. At the time I thought that wasn't so bad but soon I started to understand how serious this illness would be. Of all the care I'd received over the many years, the most important element I believed which helped me at those crucial times was the communication with my doctors and family. I knew there were people I could call upon to answer my questions and to get the information I needed but growing up, I did feel as if I was being cheated. I felt I was being robbed of my childhood as there were so many things I wanted to do but couldn't. The reason: I was either in hospital or just too sick to take part.

That was devastating.

Mum was great since she'd make those days out to the hospital seem like day trips. We'd jump on the train, have fun and Mom would always treat me to something nice like a Cadbury sweet or warm soup on those cold days. The older I became, the more I understood what was happening. The closer the hospital appointment approached, the more uncertain I was of what would happen or be said when we got there and I so wanted to escape the ward as fast as I possibly could so that I could return to school for the afternoon session, no matter how tired I felt.

On the street, nobody including most of my school friends, had any idea of how sick I was. Except, of course, for when I took medication and became swollen like a balloon or had long periods away from school due to surgery. At times, having renal failure made me feel so very isolated and though my family and friends were doing their best to be sympathetic and understanding; they'd no idea what I was feeling or going through. My parents had done all they could do to help, trying to fight it but unfortunately there was not much more that they could have done.

At my hospital appointments, I knew every test that could possibly be taken to determine what was causing my kidneys to fail but they always turned up negative and that was hard to deal with. A very rough road to walk. It was after the many tests and one hospital appointment when I was told by my nephrologist that I'd need help with my kidneys. It was NOW official; they were no longer working. This also meant I'd now need to use a dialysis machine or receive a transplant to stay alive. At the time, I'd no idea what that meant but I do remember thinking it was going to be a massive hindrance to me. I began thinking that death was surely a much better outcome. It was upsetting hearing about my condition and yet worse was to come. Eventually we found out that due to the advancement of my disease, my kidneys would fail.

When I was first diagnosed, I felt massive amounts of anger towards my doctors, even though I knew it wasn't their fault. I hated myself and kept asking, *Did I deserve this?*

After a number of surgeries and the scars became more prominent, I hated what I saw whenever I looked in a mirror. My entire body began to change and being short with a big belly, I despised the way I looked. What was interesting was that I did not fall into any of the categories of persons at risk of renal failure since nobody in my family suffered from it. So I wondered where it came from and how I'd become afflicted with it? I just couldn't understand. I thought all sickness came from a source; that is passed from one family member to the next and it was very difficult for me to accept this is now my reality. A reality without an origin.

This was now my life and it took time for me to reach a place of acceptance; once I had, I began to feel better.

Unfortunately, that feeling wouldn't last too long.

Chapter 2 – Why Was I Different?

When I was first diagnosed with renal failure I was far too young to really understand what was happening but I do remember being shielded by my parents, maybe to hide me from what was really going on. I know they tried to let me have as normal a life as possible. At times I wanted to do things I knew I shouldn't be doing but still, they allowed me even for a few moments to play or eat something I shouldn't, until those times when my childhood was ripped away from me without offering me a choice. As a child I faced adversity that seemed like a nightmare and I just wanted to start my life again. Unfortunately, going into my teens, I was left with deeper, longer-lasting scars than I care to admit and though you'd see me smiling and probably thinking I was fine, my insides were really sinking and doing so very fast.

I remembered thinking no person should experience my pain or any other horrible tragedy which may rob them of their childhood. I hated going to hospital appointments because it was there I'd see other children going through the same situation as myself; thinking nobody could help. Even though you may not identify with kidney failure, I know that at some stage in your life, you've been through something that made you who you are today - good or bad.

Ever since coming to terms with my condition, my experiences enabled me to be stronger, find a never-say-die attitude to the point where I'd normalise my hospital experiences and its environment for the betterment of myself.

I learnt a lot about painful and trauma-invoking experiences and soon realised I was made of much stronger stuff than I thought, we often are, and all it takes is the right or wrong opportunity to bring it out. Having being diagnosed with Chronic Renal Failure from I was young, I began taking a lot of medication, resulting in other medical complications that caused me to become even more anxious and scared. I never felt I had the power since my entire life was either controlled by surgery or medication. I just kept thinking this was no way for me to live, *Why was I so different from the other children in my class or immediate surroundings?*

The only time I ever felt some sort of normality was on the days when I went to hospital, since all the other children there were just like me. Whenever a child went through any medical intervention, most times this would be misunderstood since they internalised the pain and suffering; as for me, I started questioning and believing I'd done something to cause the pain.

Staying in hospital was stressful and I needed to find a way of deal with it and I soon became accustomed to it. There were many times, once my family left me alone in hospital, I'd pull the curtains around my bed and just cry, wishing to be normal and at home. As I lay there, I'd wonder what mum was cooking or what my Dad and brother were doing at that time. And the more I thought of their 'normality', the more I cried. Having this condition was not easy on my family or on me since I hated missing out on school, the trips, football training and matches. I missed my childhood fun and I felt so alone, as if I was the only one struggling with this disease.

On walking into the Great Ormond Street Hospital, one of the world's best hospitals for children, I thought this place was so big. Looking around, at times, I'd become so used to the place thinking "I'm home". As I became older and understood what was going on, it didn't seem as scary as before. I began to enjoy my visits. It was a beautifully decorated building that was nice to be in since it could've also been an old and depressing no child wanted to spend long periods of time.

I'd met an amazing doctor, Doctor Trumpeter, who looked after me and taking me under his wing, he let me: 'know that no matter what I'd go through, he was there to support me'. He had a way of knowing when he dropped a ton of bricks on you but would try to put you at ease. He'd often explained the need for and importance of kidneys as well the sort of treatment required to help me. With his support, we also knew that it was only a matter of time before I'd start dialysis. He tried reassuring me and said that I'd be able to live a fairly normal life as long as I had regular dialysis, took my prescribed medicine and followed my renal diet.

Many times I didn't want to believe what I'd heard about the treatment, impending surgery, medication or diet, especially as I just wanted to be and live my life. Often times, I thought perhaps my condition was not as bad as they were making it sound or out to be. I'd think that perhaps my blood results had got mixed up with someone else's; maybe I was just having a nightmare and I'd soon wake up with two good kidneys and all this would be over…. but the reality of my situation began to sink in. How would I deal with it? I'd no idea but felt anger and cheated and kept asking: **"Why ME?"**

As I grew older, I asked more questions. *What kind of changes would kidney failure make in my life? What activities would I need to give up? Would I be able to continue as normal, would I even want to? What foods could I no longer be allowed to eat? What medicine and how much would I need to take?* I was drifting and drifting because I couldn't see any light at the end of this tunnel. This time, was a time of total confusion. *How would I deal with it?*

I found myself, health-wise, in a place I'd never been before and this brought a natural fear and the question of whether anybody would truly accept me for me and not as some sort of charity case, kept coming to mind. *Would I ever be able to accomplish what I'd like to accomplish and if I could stay alive long enough how would I face the prospect of marriage?*

With all that, there was only one way to cope with my fear of the unknown and that was to get to know what I'd need to know. The more one knew, starting out, the better one could be prepared for what awaited. So, my journey continued...

Chapter 3 – Princess Di and I

So the day came when I finally needed to start dialysis. Receiving the letter to come in for a tour and speak to the nurses who would be looking after me, caused me to freeze. I realised then that things were about to change for the worse for me and having to travel to London three times a week for treatment just seemed so daunting. **Why me?** But, I also knew, it was just another step in my journey.

Although I knew I needed to start treatment since there was no other option with half of my remaining kidney left (that'd even stopped working), I was fearful and knew there was more to come like more surgery which I always tried to avoid because of the fear that had come over me.

To know I'd be tied to a machine, three times a week, I was angry at life and everybody because it was so unfair. However, I soon realised I could never "go back" and decided to look ahead which was extremely hard to do.

My life became very different and difficult.

Balancing the medication, hospital visits and blood tests had become a way of life and after a while, once I began my dialysis, it was at least a step to a normal life and as much as I could I had to think positive.

In this situation, I found the most-needed quality for success was to have the right attitude to my illness although sometimes I failed dramatically but didn't allow it to get the better of me. Even so, I knew I'd never give up.

Dialysis wasn't an emotionally smooth ride. At times I'd go into the dialysis unit, making jokes and speaking to the friends I'd made in the hospital, including the nurses. I'd then go the other extreme where I wouldn't care if nobody spoke to me and I just wanted to be left alone. At times it got to the point where I was tired of always smiling and acting as if everything was fine, because it wasn't. I was missing out on so much either at home with my family, school, after school, hanging out and playing football – so, I wasn't okay. I'd have days when something small would set me off or I'd fall back into grieving for the life I had before starting dialysis. After all, it was a big life change and an unwanted one. I didn't ask for this and didn't want it. Surely death would've been a better option for me.

After a while the treatment plus the travelling to and from the hospital got to me and I felt my life was spiralling out of control and there was nothing I could do about it. Coming from a Christian upbringing I was taught that God would always help me and never gave anyone more than they could bear but at times I thought that was a lie because most days it felt I was carrying way more than I was capable of. The funny thing was, people kept telling me I was so strong to carry what I was carrying but they knew nothing of how my insides were being crushed and I just wanted to escape.

It wasn't until I was around 13, 14 years old and made a friend in Great Ormond Street that I realised some important things.

Mandeep was his name and we quickly became very good friends. He was one of the very few people who I could relate with and who knew where I was coming from. I guess you could say we met for a reason and that was for him to shine a light on my darkest hour. If I ever saw him again, I'd want to say: *"Thank you for showing me another way. Not to take every day so seriously when dealing with renal failure. It's OK to smile and still have fun."*

We both had the same issue and even when our treatment became unbearable, we somehow made it work for us, to the point where we became known in the renal and dialysis unit as two trouble makers. And our friendship began in the hospital and continued outside it too. I won't forget when Mandeep left because he finally received a transplant and a feeling of emptiness came over me because of the few years we were locked in together. We became like brothers and that was taken away from me. Although we spoke and I was so happy for him, I became fearful of the unknown, how was I now going to cope without him? And even though my other friends and the nurses were great, he actually understood me.

During my early teens at Great Ormond, I was scared of the unknown. I didn't know what my future looked like and I'd be scared of what they were going to tell me every time I went for an appointment. But I held onto what my dear friend, Mandeep, had told me and learnt as he was always so positive even though, at the time, we were going through what we were going through. He'd encouraged me to look at my situation completely differently and helped to change my mindset. After a while I knew and believed this was not going to beat me, I didn't know how or even when but I knew I needed to dig deep, fighting every day to stay alive.

Many times I lived in denial. I'd deny I had renal failure and I'd be more competitive at sports, playing harder, sometimes putting my body on the line. I became extremely gung-ho as I wanted to show the rest of my peers I was the same as them. So I pushed everything to the limit but then paid for it afterwards since when I reached home, I was either so tired or in pain. At the time of playing I wouldn't admit that my kidneys weren't working or my life had changed because of them. I'd always tell my friends not to take it easy with me because of my health but to treat me like they would a normal person and play hard.

Although the journey was long and hard it was because of it I had the honour of meeting the late Princess Diana of Wales. I remembered going into the dialysis centre one day and my nurses were telling me what was going to happen. Everybody was so excited and on that day it felt like the dialysis unit was a bit different because this special lady was coming in to see us. I remembered when she walked over to my side room. At first I couldn't believe how tall and beautiful she was. She spoke with such elegance; you could tell she cared about every individual. When she spoke to me, I forgot all about where I was and why I was there. Though our meeting was brief, I remembered her telling me to hold on and never give up. From our little meeting and that day onwards, I was able to draw on my strength. Thanks to the late Princess Di.

Chapter 4 - Transition

It's funny how life can be when you're just getting used to something and then suddenly, things begin to change...

I remembered getting to the age when I was used to things around me and I was told I needed to move hospitals as Great Ormond Street was just for children up to the age of sixteen. This came as a major shock to me since I didn't want to leave. It became my home. I knew the place, the doctors and nurses and it was almost impossible for me to think I wouldn't be going to that hospital anymore and would have to begin the entire process all over again. The staff and I had become very close and it felt like everybody who I had come to rely on was being taken away from me. I became uncomfortable and the upcoming change felt worse than a rug being pulled from underneath me.

In some kind of weird way, I felt rejected. It was like they no longer wanted me, at a time when I needed them the most. Great Ormond Street was all I knew and was accustomed to, and as much as I knew the hospital was for children and had helped me, I knew the day would've come to move on, that was still very painful to deal with. I knew at some point I needed to prepare myself and this was more challenging than the actual health issue I was facing. What made it worse, the timing of it all was not good since I was facing many health setbacks. I'd come to trust the staff and wasn't interested in getting to know any new doctors or nurses as much as the Great Ormond staff tried convincing me about the change.

Sometimes things come into our lives over which we've no control and they may either make or break us. It was down to us to make the right choices and this took a while for me to learn. I needed to remind myself that this was a process I needed to go through especially since I'd spent my childhood at this amazing hospital, growing up there and seeing many changes. I felt like I owed the doctors and nurses who'd done so much for me, who'd got me to where I was able to accept my health condition.

I'd be transferred to The Royal Free Hospital which was also in London but I'd never heard of this place and I didn't know anybody there. Would the staff like me and me them? All types of questions needed answering and yet, looking back, some of those questions were just silly because it didn't matter if they liked me or not, they were there to keep me alive.

At Great Ormond Street, I was very much sheltered from a lot to do with my illness and that transition meant I'd be more involved, taking more responsibility for my treatment options and the way my health condition needed to be managed. I considered the move before talking to my consultant as I was fast approaching eighteen. I would've liked to have been informed a bit earlier and possibly even have met the new staff beforehand and though I was very upset and had many negative memories it was a really smooth transition. It felt I'd moved at the right time.

As a child I was always very inquisitive, so I wouldn't let the doctors just speak to my mum alone. I'd make sure I was asking questions so I always knew what was going on and what to expect. But I made things very difficult for my new doctor and nurses especially as I really didn't want to be there. I didn't know what to expect and made judgments about them way before. I just didn't know if the treatment would be better than what I'd received at Great Ormond

Street which I know sounds a bit corny but it was one of…if not the best hospital in the country.

We've all heard those horror stories about adult hospitals but they weren't true and the first time I went to The Royal Free was like going to a new school but also a feeling of heading into the unknown. My first impressions of the Royal Free were that it was a clean, friendly and a welcoming hospital, a bit like my previous hospital. The staff was smiling and understood where I was coming from and my reservations about attending a new hospital were taken on board. But still, I really missed the Great Ormond staff and the treatment I received there, and even though the new Royal Free staff were doing all they could to make me feel welcome, it just didn't feel the same.

I felt the difference as the doctors and nurses dealt directly with me instead of talking to my parents about me and I was more involved in the decisions. After a while, it seemed that moving there gave me a real sense of independence and responsibility as it related to my appointments.

I understand some of you may be in a period of transition and struggling or even worried but take courage. Transition may be very painful but if there's a good support network around you, it can be done. The main thing I would say is just keep your head held high, be confident and look forward no matter what challenges may come your way. It will be a new experience and worth it in the long run.

Chapter 5 – Bad and Good News

I was getting used to being at the new hospital and the staff was getting familiar with me. Things were fine. Every kidney patient wishes for the freedom of having a transplant and unfortunately nobody knows how long that wait will be. At times, this was very painful for me. With kidney transplants happening all the time waiting for that phone call to hear a kidney was available, brought phenomenal joy.

I remembered the night when we got the phone call. I was at home, getting ready for bed when we received it.

A kidney became available and it was one of the very few times I didn't mind being awakened in the early hours of the morning since I knew that in the next few days my life would change and I could have it back. I remembered them telling my mum they'd found a match and it was a very good one. My family needed to get me to the hospital as soon as possible so everything was frantic with bag-packing, getting a shower and dropping my brother off at my grandmother's house since it was late at night and he had school the following day. Everything was time sensitive and it felt like I was in a movie, playing someone else since I couldn't believe my time had finally come and I had a chance to get my life back on track, dialysis free and living like a normal person.

Due to having renal failure, I'd become quite anxious about things, struggling to just enjoy being in the moment. I kept thinking something would go wrong and kept considering the "what ifs" and with so many setbacks, when it was time to go, and I was in the car everything suddenly became hazy.

Everywhere seemed distant, I could see people and their mouths moving but I couldn't understand what they were saying. I remembered my Mum asking if I was ok. My heart was about to explode in my chest and I wanted to get to the hospital as soon as possible because, even though I knew the kidney was a good match, I knew there were still tests to go through and the hospital could come back and say the operation was not going ahead. So I didn't want to get too excited until they actually confirmed the operation would go ahead.

The anxious feeling was horrible because I knew there was nothing I could do if it didn't happen and the more I thought about it, the more I panicked. I didn't say anything to my parents as we drove to the hospital but they knew I was nervous and kept telling me it was going to be fine. It got to the point where I didn't even want to talk and just wanted to be left alone.

When we got to the hospital, it was so quiet. The corridors were empty and an eerieness made me feel even worse. I began to feel uncertain I could go through with the operation. But I was so glad for the support of my parents since if it wasn't for them, I would've probably talked myself out of going through with it.

We arrived on the ward early in the morning, when all of the patients were asleep. The nurses were so happy to see me. I remembered one asking me so many questions. It was all exciting but I knew there were tests coming before I'd even got to the operating theatre. Even so, I learnt that through the entire process, I needed to take my emotions out of it and the moment came when the nurses began asking all the medical questions and told me not to eat anything since if the tests were good, the operation would occur within a few hours. The tests comprised blood tests, scans, an x-ray and a CT scan. Every test took so long, I was tired and just wanted to sleep and tried pretending it wasn't happening. I just wanted to go home but my parents were reassuring and telling me to keep calm. It wasn't easy.

With the tests completed, the Transplant Team told me to get some rest and that they'd let me know as soon as possible if the operation would go ahead. When they left, I remembered looking at the clock and it felt as if it'd stood still and whenever there was a knock on the door, I'd be a little bit nervous, my heart beating fast, pacing back and forth as I thought: *'Please let me have some good news. Please let this operation go ahead because I am so tired mentally and physically, and just need a break'*.

The hours began to pass and I hadn't heard anything and so many thoughts went through my head as I said the operation wasn't going to happen. My brother also crossed my mind as I wondered how he was doing and whether he was okay. I hoped he wouldn't hate me for leaving him behind and wished he was with me.

In my head, I kept saying sorry to him for having my illness and having left him on his own. I said maybe his and my parent's life would've been better if I wasn't around but then I remembered how he had my back and wanted nothing but the best for me. I felt bad. When we were growing up, I was the one who'd received the attention but never once had he complained, judged or knocked me down for it. He'd always been supportive.

I heard voices outside my room door, it was the nurses and the transplant surgeons. I thought: *Ok let's get ready for the bad news.* They entered and woke up my parents. The surgeons were so cool and said it was fine, we were going to do the operation. I won't forget their smiles; it was a happy ending to a living nightmare. I was ready to go.

My parents were on either side of my bed, my Mother not letting go of my hand as I was wheeled to theatre. At this point she was also nervous, though she never said. Finally, we got to the point of no return and the nurses said my parents couldn't go any further, they both gave me a kiss and said they'd see me soon. I was so nervous, an emotional wreck and there was a lump in my throat. I couldn't speak. I just knew that if I spoke, there'd be a flood of tears but, instead, I gave them a wave and whispered I'd see them soon.

I recalled going into the room. It was freezing cold with very bright white lights and loads of medical equipment around. Nurses were around too, preparing everything to put me to sleep. People were coming in and out and I thought my heart was going to stop. My blood pressure was so high they tried keeping me calm but I knew I was at a crucial time in my life, again I was thinking of my brother, hoping he was fine and my parents would now get some rest. I drifted off to sleep and the last words I heard were: *"Here we go"*.

When I woke I'd have my life back...with no more dialysis.

Chapter 6 – The Struggle Is Real

In a soft whisper I asked, "Is the kidney working?"

Those were the first words that came from my mouth when I awoke…but instead of seeing smiles, I saw my Mum in tears, barely able to talk. I watched her as she walked towards me, leant over and said in her soft voice, "I'm sorry son, it didn't work."

Right then a dark cloud came over me and I burst into tears because I realised all the dreams I'd had the day before were no longer possible. In the room, my parents tried their best to help me gain my composure but my tears flowed till I drifted back to sleep. The anaesthetic was still in my system and it made me weak. When I was awake again, I just started to cry and even when my friends and people from our local church visited, I'd no interest in seeing them or anybody else. I just wanted to be left alone.

The surgeon came and saw me and what he said next really made me angry. He explained that even before stirring from the surgery, they'd returned me to theatre to remove the kidney because they'd found an infection. I was livid because, to me, it seemed that the entire procedure had been a waste of time. In my mind, I questioned why I allowed myself to even go through the experience, especially as the thought of renal failure or another transplant made me fearful. Now, all I wanted to do was just die. The feelings of failure and rejection were so painful to accept. How could my life go from a point of excitement to not even wanting to live? Nothing made any sense anymore and I was close to giving up.

Sometimes, in life, things happen that seem unfair and not right but we need to somehow battle through with the tears in our eyes and on bended knee. We must fight. For me, at this point I was full of bitterness and anger, but somehow, one day I will have to recover and get back in the fight.

I had many visitors and when they spoke I wasn't listening, their words, going through one ear and out the other. I came from a Christian family and my father was the Pastor of a church, so many people would visit, trying to encourage me to stay strong in God but I didn't want to hear anything about that - who was this God you talked to me about that would allow me to go through such pain? What had I done to deserve such a bad hand in this life? Is this the God you talked to me about? I was just not interested.

The doctor eventually advised me not to go back on the kidney transplant list for a little while since he knew I wasn't mentally ready but truth be told, I didn't care.

In life, most of us have been rejected at some point. It is a part of life. You like a boy or girl but for some reason he/she does not feel the same way you do. That kind of rejection I can understand but this felt so much more hurtful and no matter what I did, the ache would never leave me.

Over time the scar from the surgery healed but I still carried a much bigger scar. My mental, emotional and physical being were in poor shape. This was a very hard blow for me and my family to accept. How was I going to return to school and tell my friends that the kidney did not work? Would they laugh at me? How would people look at me now, when before, they looked at me as some sort of soldier but now they'll realise I was only human, after all. I thought that maybe I was being judged by God or he was trying to get my attention and if he was, this wasn't the way to do it. As far as I was concerned, the last thing I needed to was hear about

God, Christianity or the church. My Dad was a pastor, after all, and sold out for God, so why would He allow this to happen to my family? It was not fair.

I didn't have the answers but I knew I was scared of what was to come. Out of all the times we suffered some sort of rejection, this particular one hit us the hardest. It was all too much for me and I was left wondering: *how could life be so cruel?* This was probably the first time I needed to face my illness head-on since previously, when I was younger, I'd been protected from the gravity of it all by my family. Now older, I thought I couldn't expect them to protect me anymore.

Some of the worst rejections happen when we are young because our hearts are still too pure, and unaccustomed to being denied what we want.

I felt that I was too young to deal with such an issue: I'd built the courage to go through with the surgery but within a few hours, I was in deep emotional pain, which would stick with me for many years to come. Somehow, it robbed me of my life, joy and peace of mind; my head had become a battlefield.

How I Survived 5 Kidney Transplants and Won!

I was never a 'normal' child, so fast forward over a decade, when this transplant came up and I thought I was finally going to be normal and do normal things. Instead, I was yet again robbed and cheated. It was like life was constantly having a laugh at me with my battle after battle, each one harder than the one before. Here I was, trying to plan my next five years and what I was going to do, places I wished to visit and so on, but now, because of my situation, this wasn't going to happen.

The time came when I had to return to school. I didn't want to because I would have to explain what had happened to people who really didn't know about my issue. The walk to school was so long that along the way, I tried thinking about what I was going to say. I panicked and began to walk even slower and though there was so much going on in my head, walking felt good. In all my anxiety, I knew my family was worried about me since I wasn't the same person as before. My character had changed.

I was late and when I arrived, my class had already started. I lingered outside for a while because I didn't want to go in. I was so nervous. But my teacher came outside and gave me the biggest smile ever; she said: "Darren, you're back!"

She gave me a huge hug and told me to come into class with her and it would be alright. All my friends were sitting there and for a split second it felt like time stood still. Then, I heard: "Dazza's back". Everyone was so happy to see me and that made me feel so comfortable, my negative thoughts vanishing for the time I was there. My friends asked me so many questions and when I told them the kidney hadn't worked, I made jokes out of it, just to be 'one of the lads' but the pain I felt was so overwhelming I wanted to weep. I quickly changed the subject. I had made up my mind that I wasn't going to cry in front of them.

Just as I was getting back into the groove at school, it was lunchtime which meant one thing: football with my friends. I was asked but remembered I wasn't allowed to, my mum making sure to tell my teachers. So everyone watched me and even at school, the restrictions were there which really didn't help. Everybody had my best interest at heart but there were times I just wanted to run and scream. I just wanted people to accept me as I was but this didn't happen. It even got to the point where my friends were so overprotective that they wouldn't allow me to play. I could go nowhere and just be normal. I understood but I just wanted to be left alone and if I injured myself at least it would allow me to be me.

One day after school I was walking home with a friend, we were talking about my health because she wanted to understand. It was getting late and as I finished my ice-cream, she asked if she could see my scars. I never liked my scars so I laughed it off and tried to talk about something else but she wouldn't let up. So I showed her. She looked at me with her eyes filling with tears; she said, "I'd never guessed you carried so much." Little did she know that I was dying inside, screaming out for help.

She became a very good friend though and every morning, we walked to and from school and just talked. I never really knew what was going on in her head though and when she asked me questions, it was nice that someone just took the time to show they cared.

I don't think I really ever got over what happened since it set me back in so many ways. If it wasn't for the support and love of my parents and brother I don't think I would've made it. Even though it was so many years ago, it still haunts me and when people see me laughing they don't realize that underneath there are so many questions some of which may never be answered.

Have you ever been so in pain that you wanted the world to stop? It's not until you've reached that point that you can know just how deeply you can feel. At times we try to brush off a person's emotions but can we really judge so severely the intensity and truthfulness of those feelings in their time of trouble? The intensity can go away but it can also last a lifetime and we just have to learn to adapt.

When I lost the kidney, I saw how it put a strain not only on me but my whole family. It was about taking one day at a time but somehow, that was easier said than done. My brother had to see his younger sibling struggle and fight every single day of his life, get so close to an opportunity of freedom, and have it ripped from his hands. He became very quiet and though he could not understand, it never once came between us. I don't think we even really spoke about it as he saw I was suffering and he just wanted to support me even more than before. He became my rock when I couldn't stand.

We all had our own individual battles to fight and get over.

Although Mum and Dad were committed to church and never lost hope or faith it was hard for them to come to terms with what had happened with me. My Mum was very emotional and cried a lot and became a shadow of her truer self and because I was in a very dark place, I was very bitter and somewhat twisted, extremely angry with my health, doctors and life to the point of giving up. Dad, struggled with it all, albeit internally, he held the family together. He would always give a word of encouragement, he always said God would bring us through and things would get better.

A part of me was angry with Mum and Dad for being so committed to God and taking us to church because I would sit there with everything going through one ear and out the other. I kept thinking this God you were talking about, if he controlled all things, he would've allowed the kidney to work but instead he made me and my family suffer. I really didn't want to be in the church at all and had made up my mind that once I was old enough to make my own decisions, I'd leave since it had nothing to offer me. I respected my parents so much though, because not once did they judge or look down on me. All they said was that they'd pray for me that things would change. They were always so supportive. We all knew that this was big for the family and I would need a miracle but we didn't know where it would come from. Before I knew it, my life was spiraling out of control.

Sometimes the cruelest thing was not knowing what actually went wrong. All I wanted was a kidney, to live life, be a young person and explore life but this illness, time after time kept setting me back, surely death would be an easier option. I thought that I was burdening my family and didn't want to see them hurt. Maybe, with me out of the way, life would be better for my family. Even my mother was ill with cancer, so I thought what more could my family take. It was just not right. It wasn't fair. Why should my parents have to deal with cancer and a sick child? God, where were you when we needed you most?

I felt completely abandoned and despite my family being around me, it was one the longest and loneliest journeys I've ever taken in my life. Of course, there are some aspects of yourself that you can't change, like the sound of your voice, the way we walk or how we express ourselves when we talk. We make peace with the fact that we can't change these attributes and we move on. But when you don't know why we are the way we are, you just spend days, weeks or even years wondering: "What did I do wrong?"

Chapter 7 – Being Thankful

So it finally came to a point where, after losing my kidney, that I really needed to start the rebuilding process and accept what was - the kidney hadn't worked and I was back on dialysis and not even on the transplant list. All of this was very hard to take but it was the situation I found myself in and I just needed to get on with it. This process is never easy as it required a lot of work, confronting and determination, even when I didn't feel like I wanted to.

What if, one day you woke up and decided you were tired of feeling tired and had enough of everything? Enough of the stress and anxiety. Enough of the anger and resentment. Enough of the struggle, lack and pain. Enough of crying yourself to sleep, heartbreak and self-destructive thoughts. What if you just decided you wanted to change yourself, change the way you thought? We may not be able to change the situation we are in but we may change the way we thought about and looked at the situation.

I remembered, when I came to terms with losing the kidney after just eight hours, I asked God to help me because there was no way I was capable of doing it on my own. Everything about me needed to change, my relationship with God needed to grow because I wished for him to lead and guide me every step of the way since I knew without God in my life I would've been dead a long time ago.

It got to a point where I spent so much time hating myself and thinking had I done something to lose the kidney in such a short space of time. A part of me felt very guilty because someone had died, leaving me their kidney but it hadn't worked. I hated looking at myself in the mirror. Was I a horrible and bad person? But my doctors kept telling me it was one of those things that happened and there was nothing I could've done and one day I would get that working kidney. That took a long time for me to accept. I needed to forget it, release and let go of my attachment to any past struggles and allow every challenge in my way to make me better not bitter.

For me the first thing I needed to do was thank God every day that I was alive and the situation hadn't killed me. I became extremely grateful when I looked around at the people I had in my life. My family was my rock and supported me through a very difficult period and for me, without God and my family life, things would've been very different. So I made a commitment to let go of what was behind me because I couldn't change the past. I started to appreciate what was in front of me.

Let me encourage you: if your life is falling apart around you, in any area, please just trust the process. Through the darkest times in our lives a light will shine forth although it may take a while for us to see.

At times life can be unfair and we find ourselves in very difficult, trying situations but we need to know that at the end of the day, we will win.

At times we think God will deliver us out of every situation but the truth is, he won't. Sometimes he will walk us through, we may shed some tears or feel pain but know there will never be a time nor place for those who believe in God when he will leave you alone.

When I made up my mind to rebuild my life and get back to normality, it felt good that I was doing something positive, though at times it felt draining. I recall returning to my education and everybody was so happy to see me and telling me how strong I was, to go through what I went through. What they didn't know was the pain I was feeling through my smile. Where I was looking for help, others were drawn to my strength which I found so strange. Especially as I was dying inside but people were encouraged by my story.

If you are going to rebuild your life, you will need to lose the negativity.

I wouldn't allow any negative words or people around me because I knew I was going through a process.

Though many years had passed I remember having a hospital appointment and it was time to move to another hospital because now as an adult, I was moving to Milton Keynes Renal Unit. It was a frightening experience since I didn't know anybody but in my mind I was stronger and was willing to start a new journey. At the unit, I was introduced to a new consultant and he was exactly who I needed, he was a very straight talker. I remember him telling me in one appointment: "If you want to live or die let me know so I know what to do with you."

Hearing a consultant talk so directly was new to me because nobody had talked to me like that before but it was now time to take responsibility for my actions; my health, my treatment and my life. Over the years there were many conversations.

How I Survived 5 Kidney Transplants and Won!

We saw things differently at times but he had and continues to play a major part in my life. He had always been real with me and though at times when he had, I got angry deep down I knew he was telling the truth. On the other hand, when I'd been seriously ill, he came running to make sure I was fine and to check if there was anything that could be done.

I owe him so much and am so grateful to have him in my life.

I got to a place where I could forgive myself for my past actions, hurting my loved ones and learnt to live even on dialysis. Being three times a week, tied to a machine was not easy but it was possible because I knew somehow I would not be in that situation forever and even on my bad days, God was keeping me, my family and the nurses were supporting me through it all.

I had to start small and trust that as I worked on letting go of all the extra baggage weighing me down, I began to feel lighter and gained a lot more clarity over my life. I felt happier and more at peace with the world around me.

Shifting my focus from the bad to the good, from the pain to gain, from resentment to forgiveness, gratitude, and appreciation; I learnt to embrace with grace all that I faced having a sheer determination not to quit.

I say appreciate everything life sends your way, whether good or bad and know: *"Gratitude makes sense of our past, brings peace for today, and creates a vision for tomorrow."* ~ Melody Beattie

I thank God for being my peace when everything around me was crumbling, the storms raging and when nothing at times made sense and nobody understood the pain. I felt God was always there. Sometimes we need to be patient and gentle with ourselves while working on rebuilding our lives, remembering to enjoy the journey.

Chapter 8 – Finding 'The One'!

I think one of the hardest things for a patient with any sickness is finding genuine relationships that'll last, finding someone who'll accept you for who you are and not out of pity. It's a very challenging thing to find real love and it's something most people crave; to be loved and to be accepted.

Personally it was very challenging. Although I had an outgoing personality, sometimes I would be in a room full of people and still feel alone. I often wondered how I'd find someone when I had such a serious illness and didn't know when it would end. I was on a machine three times a week and had a body full of scars which brought up other issues such as my insecurity, negative emotions and my dislike of what I saw in the mirror. I often thought if I didn't even like what I saw how would someone else?

Often when we're insecure in our own skin, we try to find acceptance in someone else which could cause us trouble because of the potential to get involved in a relationship we shouldn't be in or we didn't even want to be in. Then, not only do we cause pain to ourselves but to the other person who has invested their time and emotion in us. The bad thing about all this? We rush into a relationship and yet still feel alone. The truth? No person will ever complete you if you're still a broken mess. This was one of the hardest things for me to personally accept.

Often when people want a new relationship, they either look for someone to complete them or they imagine sharing their life with someone just like them. So they try to present themselves in the best possible light for their imagined future partner - either as one perfect half of a whole or as an ideal version of what they believe their future partner would want.

When I was at one of my lowest points, I remembered hurting the people closest to me...my family. Things became just too much. When I was living at home, I went through a very rebellious stage and wanted to do my own thing I knew I loved my family very much but something wasn't registering. I ended up leaving my parents' house and my life took a spiral out of control.

Growing up, I'd lived quite a sheltered life. I had not been exposed to certain things but when I left home, I found myself with a group of people who I thought were my friends.

How I Survived 5 Kidney Transplants and Won!

I started dating a girl and that was nothing but hell on earth. I ended up living with her sister and remembered sitting in my room wondering what on earth was going on? How did I end up here? Going from a beautiful home to this place? I would often think about what my parents and brother would be doing or what they were having for dinner. It was heartbreaking to know that because of my decisions and actions, I'd found myself in this predicament. Many times I'd go to bed and I didn't want to see the morning. I hated my life and what it had become. I knew these people weren't really my friends and I felt like I'd walked into a trap. Importantly, I knew that if I ever became sick I'd be pretty much left to die. What would happen to me? Who would I call if something went wrong with my health?

I knew, then, it was time to leave and make things right with my family.

I knew the people who'd been there from day one, would always be there. I felt terrible. I questioned, how I could have treated them so badly when they had done nothing wrong.

I was so nervous returning home but what surprised me...I was welcomed like nothing had happened. Up to this day I love my family and would do anything for them since I know the journey we've all been on. Many people may see us but have no idea where our journey began or when some very dark days were upon us. I am forever indebted to them for all they've done for me.

When I was growing up as a young guy, I'd jumped from relationship to relationship looking for acceptance, looking for someone to heal my pain but this was never achieved. Instead of just having a good friend, it often went into a relationship when that was the last thing I needed. It was something I wanted but it wouldn't do me any good since the hard truth was, back then, what I had to offer any woman was broken. I didn't even know what love was. I was a mess and needed to take the time to sort myself out.

Being brought up in a Christian home, I'd often hear and read this scripture:

Matthew 6:33 (KJV): But seek ye first the kingdom of God, and his righteousness; and all these things shall be added unto you.

Back then, this scripture made no sense to me but over time I asked: 'God, what does this mean? Why do I get into relationships and often say "this is the one" but yet it breaks down?' I realised, then, that this scripture made perfect sense. I needed to sort me out first since my most important relationship was not with my parents, not my brother or the girl in my life at that time but with God.

My life was a mess. My health was a mess and instead of turning to God, I was running to a woman when that was the last thing I needed to do. Now as I was getting older, I thought it was time to sort my life out with God, asking him to forgive me for all the pain I had caused people, especially within my family. I realised, I was going through a process and this was all part of my journey.

Often times I gave credit to my relationships when I was doing fine but the truth was without God I would've been dead a long time ago. It was He who held me up. It was He who kept me going when I wished to give up.

Being in a relationship is not a bad thing since we all want to give love and feel loved and be appreciated, but when we're not mentally prepared for it, it may destroy us. That was what was happening to me, it was destroying me. What I needed to do was stay single and focus on me but that was easier said than done.

Proverbs 18:22 (KJV) Whoso findeth a wife findeth a good thing, and obtaineth favour of the LORD.

I was living on my own at this point and getting on with my life. I really felt like I'd turned a corner but the burning question came up - would I ever find true love?

I had enough of jumping from relationship to relationship and didn't want to hurt anybody because I'd actually met some great people. Many times I felt badly about how my past relationships ended and would return to the partner saying how sorry I was for the part I played, truly sorry because it wasn't them, it had been me.

So, after a two-year relationship ended, I stopped looking for "The One" and decided to turn my attention inward, to get to know and accept myself, healing my past wounds. Previously, I needed to be with someone in order to feel content, to have someone love me in order to feel loved. Breaking up with my past girlfriends was so painful since it felt as if I was being torn from a part of myself.

I discovered, I needed to learn to be whole. And when I started to work on that, my life changed.

As time went on, I met a lady. We'd always been friends and got on very well, she was the complete opposite to who I'd normally be attracted to and in the past I thought that was a bad thing. I always thought to have or be in a successful relationship you'd need someone exactly like yourself who liked the same things but that was not the case. In some past relationships I felt like I couldn't be myself and hid the real me. I hid about my illness, putting my relationship before my health, smiling and hiding the pain and not talking about how I really felt. I knew relationships were not meant to be like that.

When I met this lady it all changed. Her name was Amanda Thomas and she was new to my world. A breath of fresh air. She was so refined, quiet and completely opposite to me. She was just beautiful, although I'd known of her for many years, at this point I looked at her and thought maybe this could work but every time we spoke, she'd always refer to me as "Stephanie's cousin," so I knew she was making a point that something couldn't happen because of this and every time I saw her, for some strange reason, I kept saying:

"You're going to be my wife," and I'm sure she thought I was crazy. I also knew I needed not only God's help but the help of my cousin to put in a good word for me!

After some time, we began to really talk and the more we spoke, the more relaxed I felt but still there were some reservations; the challenges of a committed relationship and my health… would she be able to accept me for who I was and what I was going through? But I remembered my Dad really talking to me about Amanda, telling me what he thought and felt. His advice was what I needed to hear since he knew exactly where I was coming from and what sort of person I needed to see me through this journey. It wasn't going to be easy and she needed to be special.

I won't forget that night when I called Amanda and we started talking at 7.30pm. We literally spoke for the entire night because the next thing I remember was that GMTV was on at 6.30am! I said to her, "I have to go to work." I remember that for the whole day I was so tired and thought I couldn't do that again but I spent the day with a smile on my face. In the back of my mind I knew I had liked this girl for a long time but the opportunity never truly presented itself.

How I Survived 5 Kidney Transplants and Won!

I invited Amanda to come and visit me when I was on dialysis since I wanted to see how she'd react, whether she was reticent or would embrace me in the usual way. When she came, she did not know that I was watching her and she was amazing. She was not fazed by what was going on and we continued to talk as normal, by this time, although she may not agree, I knew she saw me as more than "Stephanie's cousin".

How I was beginning to feel about Amanda I hadn't felt before and I knew, I really cared about her. We spoke about so many different things and shared different stories of our lives which made us happy or sad but we were always able to be ourselves and it felt so amazing. This was all new to me. Had I found the woman who was going to be my wife?

The time came when I was going to ask her out on an official date but I was so nervous. Had I read the signs all wrong? Were we just really good friends? In the back of my mind I knew if I'd read the signs all wrong I would've lost a really good friend, so I needed a sign. When had all this dating stuff become like an exam?

We were invited to a mutual friend's get-together and traveled in the same car. I wanted to see how we got on throughout the evening. It was perfect. We got there and talked the entire evening as everybody was having such a nice time. Amanda and I sat next to each other and I remember thinking this felt so natural being close to her and enjoying her company. The whole journey home we sat in the car together, talking. Later on we texted each other and we both said we really enjoyed the evening and I asked if I could see her again. She said yes and from then I knew I had a chance. It was amazing because every time I was with her I never thought about my illness and it hadn't mattered. She was the only person outside of my family and closest friends who made me feel like a normal person, made me feel I was accepted even with all my faults and with nothing to offer her.

What was I going to do? This was my one chance so I had to make it count. I decided to take her to see the Lion King and it was perfect although I was nervous. It was just so natural like we'd known each other for many years and I remember as the show went on we held hands. My heart beat wildly in my chest and my throat became dry, was this really happening? I'd found the girl of my dreams, the girl I'd longed for.

How I Survived 5 Kidney Transplants and Won!

Yes, we've had our ups and downs and there've been times when we thought we weren't going to make it but through it all I knew this was the woman I wanted to be my wife. I'd met a friend and fallen in love with a beautiful angel whom I'm very proud today to call my wife. Amanda Ferguson sacrificed so much for me and I'm forever grateful. Today she still makes my heart beat wildly. I often think about the time we'd met and the journey we've been on and I'm so happy that through my hardships and battles dealing with my condition, she's been there to hold my hand every step of the way. So is love real? Yes 100% but sometimes it'll come from the least expected places, so I say keep an open heart, keep an open mind, pray about it and if it really is the one and both of your hearts connect without a shadow of a doubt fellas when you see that woman... take a chance, take a risk... what's the worst thing that can happen? When I asked Amanda to marry me, I was still on dialysis, I was still very poorly but I knew this was the woman I was meant to be with. I still didn't have anything to offer her but she gave up her career and said yes and I'm so blessed to have this Angel by my side, so I say to you as I end this chapter if it can happen for me, then it definitely can happen for you.

Darren Ferguson

They say it is only in the movies that fairytales happen but I for one have experienced a fairytale in my own life with Amanda, she came into my life and changed it for the better and I promise to love this woman for the rest of my life. She has shown me such selflessness, caring and love that I've never experienced before. Amanda from my heart, thank you so much for accepting me with all my faults. I love you Baby.

Chapter 9 – The News

The one question I've asked myself many times growing up, is will I ever find peace and live a fulfilled life? Many times I've asked myself this question and maybe a part of me still asks the question. I know I will never find the answers to many questions I have but a lot of people can say that so we get up and get on with life.

As a renal patient who has had a long, hard journey I don't get excited about anything, it may be a holiday or a birthday but due to the journey I've been on, I had to teach myself to wait until the good news arrived because so often I'd build myself up and something bad would happen so I taught myself not to be excited about anything but this was something I needed to change within me. I needed to believe again. I needed to find hope again.

As a Christian, there were many times my faith in God was low since my question, my ultimate question was always why? Why did I have to suffer for so many years, why was it only I who was going through this in the family? I felt life had been very unfair and at times even attending church was like a chore and not something I really wanted to do. We'd hear so much but my life wouldn't match the sermon I was hearing, so I lost faith but still knew that at some stage, I'd need to pick myself up again.

After a period of time and because of all the complications I had in previous years, I was back on the transplant list. But we weren't getting any calls and sitting down with my Doctor who'd been with me for many years, we came to the realisation that it was unlikely I'd get the call, so we needed to explore other options and there weren't many.

We knew I needed a kidney as soon as possible as I was getting to the stage where I had enough of dialysis. I would've kept going but I was physically and mentally drained. It was my prayers every night which gave me the strength to keep going, even when I felt like I wanted to give in.

I just saw how the Lord kept me and gave me the strength when I needed it most. I had a great support system, Amanda was there to always be a rock when I felt low and my other family members helped me in a big way.

I remember going for a check-up and my doctor saying I didn't have many options and maybe I should consider asking my family and closest friends if they'd like to be tested. I just laughed as I thought he was joking around but, then, realised from looking at his face that he was serious. I said, how do you even start that conversation, 'oh good morning, can I have your kidney?' To me that sounded insane and something I wasn't prepared to do as it'd be a major sacrifice for someone and most people I knew were married and had kids. I always thought, suppose one day, one of their family members needed a kidney and they were not able to help? I didn't want to put myself or them in that position.

I carried on with the dialysis but my health was not getting better and my bones began to really struggle as they became even more brittle. So, again, my doctor called me and we had the same conversation since he knew I wasn't going to get a kidney from a deceased person. I wasn't comfortable with his advice but thought the only people I'd talk to about this were my family members. My Mum was unable to help because of a previous health issue.

I spoke to my Dad and Brother and they both agreed to be tested. I really felt sorry for my brother because he hated hospitals and because I knew what would need to be done if he was to volunteer his kidney. Unsurprisingly, he was willing to make the sacrifice and so we went ahead but to our surprise both of their blood groups were different from mine, I was shocked and thought I was the special *one* in the family. I prayed night after night asking God to help me since I didn't know what to do. I felt at a complete loss and was resigned to dialysis for the rest of my life. After a while and without me saying anything, some of my closest friends wished to be tested too but this was something I needed to think about especially since I knew the implications. Each of my friends was tested and like bowling pins they were knocked down one-by-one, at this point I knew it was over. Even if they'd passed one or even two tests, something would happen and we'd get that phonecall saying sorry we can't go any further. It was no surprise to me but still, it felt like a massive kick to my gut.

I think it got to the point where even my doctor was unsure about what to do and by then I just wanted to do dialysis for however long it would take. I would not ask anybody else or allow them to be tested. I was finding it a very emotional process and I was feeling let down each time. I didn't want to put anybody else through that.

Life can take us on a journey that we're not prepared for and little did I know that something was about to happen.

It was at church, one Sunday, after service when a friend said, "I want to give you my kidney." I must admit I thought he was crazy and I brushed him off thinking he had lost his mind. He'd said it so casually and calmly, I was sure he thought I was going to say "yeah fine, no worries". I quickly changed the subject. But he said it again with a bit more depth in his voice, so at this time I knew he was serious and didn't want to mess with him since he was bigger than me. I thought how could I stop this guy from talking such nonsense, especially as I'd made up my mind that nobody else was going to be tested. So I said we'd talk because I couldn't understand his reason for such a kind gesture. After all, he wasn't a family member and was a guy I knew and got on well with but not enough to warrant such a gift.

Why did he want to do this? Though I was not happy about it, I said yes because I knew some test would be coming back negative. I didn't get excited when any of the tests returned a positive result and I kept telling him I wasn't building his hopes up too much since this wasn't going to work. For some strange reason, he was always so positive so I was wondering whether he knew something that I didn't. He was also flying past all the tests and after a while I began to get nervous, and started to think, "Is this it?"

We got to the final test and as we went home, it was like a renewed hope better than a breath of fresh air. I was thinking, "Wow we'd actually done it." Even though, we still needed to wait for the results of the operation. A few weeks passed and I called and said to him, "It seems it isn't going to happen but I really thank you for trying." My heart was so heavy because he'd lost his wife to cancer and went the extra mile for me, when he already had other things going on in his own personal life.

In May 2011, I won't forget the day, month or year.

I was at work, sitting in my office when my mobile phone rang. I heard this voice, "Hi Darren it's the transplant team in Oxford." I felt I knew what was coming and was getting myself prepared for the disappointing news - that the last test had failed... but, then, there was a change in her voice. She started sounding so happy.

"What are you doing on the 11th August?"

I answered, "Nothing. Why?" I was beginning to think there was another test to but no…

"How would you feel about having a transplant on that day?" She said.

Everything within me froze, I was completely numb and couldn't speak. I began to cry. I couldn't scream. There were no words to explain what had just happened to me, like an out-of-body experience, I was floating. Like watching a movie, I was dumbfounded.

I told the lady. "I'm sorry, can I call you back?"

As soon as I put the phone down, I took a deep breath and began to cry. I couldn't believe this was going to happen. Leaving work, I went into my Dad's office with my family (I worked with my family and I was in one office while they were in another.

He must've thought something bad had happened to me… but these words tumbled out:

"I'm having a kidney transplant on August 11th."

"WHAT?!" Was my Dad's response. He was in complete shock and it was such a comical moment we will never forget. He looked like he had just swallowed a slice of bread too thick for his mouth. He was beside himself, unable to contain the many years of his and my frustration. At that moment, I loved him even more.

With this joy I called Lee Ferrigon and we just started laughing. We couldn't stop. When we did, I asked him if he'd spoken to the transplant team. Looking back, he was my guardian angel sent by God, to give me a new lease of life. I couldn't wait to tell Amanda and when I did she was over the moon. If my Dad was happy, Amanda was ecstatic. I swore, if music was playing she'd have been dancing out of where she was and into the middle of the street. And if I loved my parents then, I loved her even more. She'd been my rock.

After my heart rate slowed, I called the hospital back. For once I remembered what it felt like to be excited about something and still, I knew that because of my medical history, this transplant would be done at a price.

The transplant team said I'd need to undergo some treatment to prepare me to receive the kidney. I honestly had no idea what was coming but I felt the pain of the treatment was going to be worth it. For a few weeks before the transplant I'd been connected to a machine for four to six hours, three times a week and it had literally drained me of every fibre within my body. It had made me sick and tired. It had made me frustrated and impatient, and I was truly fed-up with everything and really just wanted something, anything to work. Even my prayers.

This was when it occurred to me that everybody wanted to be free, everybody wanted to experience freedom but weren't willing to pay the price for that freedom. Freedom can come at a very expensive cost and I'm not talking only about money. My freedom came but I needed to go through a very gruelling process. We don't know what is deep within us until we really have to dig deep and fight. We don't know how strong we truly are until we're in the last round of the fight. God can and will equip us but we must stand up and fight.

I knew of the complications. I knew my health wasn't the best but when my doctor wrote me a letter confirming this transplant would be done but it was a risk, I really had to sit up and count the cost - could I really do this? I couldn't go through losing another kidney. I couldn't put my donor through this ordeal after he'd just lost his wife. It took some time for me to think...really think.

And on Thursday 11th August 2011 at 1.30pm, I took the risk.

I walked to the operating theatre with my Dad and everything within me was a mess. I was so scared. There were flashbacks of waking up to a process that had not worked and there were so many what-if's. At the theatre doors, my Dad couldn't go any further. He gave me a hug and I watched as the door closed with him walking away. My heart sank. My hero, my Father couldn't do anything for me at this point and I whispered, "God my life is in your hands, please let this kidney work."

I remember the room being so cold, like a freezer. A white light beamed into my face as the nurses walked around. Frantically, I was looking around, my heart racing. A nurse came over to me and said, "Darren, you have to calm down, it's going to be OK."

I took a deep breath as she was about to administer the anaesthetic. Seated beside me she asked my name, date of birth and then slowly began to inject me with the potion and soon, I drifted off to sleep.

How I Survived 5 Kidney Transplants and Won!

Was my ordeal over? Had the Kidney transplant worked?

When I awoke I saw my family around me and the same question came up: "Did it work?" With smiles across their faces, they said yes and I'd already started to pass water. The relief I felt was indescribable and all I could do was thank God that the kidney had worked. The joy I felt knowing I had my life back was hard to explain. There'd be no more three times a week trips to the hospital and so a massive burden had been lifted from my shoulders. Looking about, everything and everyone looked so beautiful, although I was in pain from the surgery I didn't care. I remember thinking I was so hungry I could eat an entire herd of horses but settled for a slice of toast instead.

What my donor Lee Ferrigon had done for me, he will never understand. HI could never repay him and I am forever indebted to him. We have a bond which we don't even share with our beautiful ladies. We are kidney brothers; a bond I will cherish forever. As time passed before the transplant, I had made a list of all the things I wanted to do but the opportunities had not yet arisen. The first thing was to visit Las Vegas and I was so happy since I was blessed to go with Amanda. It was like a fresh start and I was so nervous about travelling since I hadn't done so in so many years. It was so good and a few years later, we went to New York and Paris - life has been great and I am so happy and content. Yes, the battle goes on to keep the kidney working but six years have passed and we're doing well and by God's grace will continue to do well.

So as I end, let me encourage you. No matter what you're facing, don't you dare quit, don't you dare give in because you're much stronger than that. You're stronger than you think you are and though it can be a very lonely road at times, never forget that God is with you and will bring you through. Just trust and believe him and know he is able and perfect in everything that's wrong in our lives.

Whatever you may be fearful about take courage and take that risky step because you never know, it may be the one step you need to take that'll change your life. If you're tired…have a rest, take a moment and think, plan your next move but when you've rested, get up and continue to fight this walk we call life. This is my fifth transplant and I'm believing God it's my final transplant and I thank God every day for this blessing.

Life's all about choices...the choices we make today will determine our tomorrows, so do you choose to lose or get up. Shake yourself off, get back in the fight and WIN!

It's *your* choice.

I'm still traveling on my journey and what'll become of it only time will tell but for now Darren and the kidney are enjoying the ride.

Darren Ferguson

How I Survived 5 Kidney Transplants and Won!

Darren Ferguson

How I Survived 5 Kidney Transplants and Won!

87

The Life of Darren Ferguson

Amanda Ferguson - Wife

Darren was always a bubbly character kind of guy, so falling in love with him was very, very easy. The way he was and still is, you could never tell that he ever had any form of sickness, so to me sickness was never a problem or reason not to want to marry the love of my life. I always believed he would be well and that this was a season that we just had to pass through. But the difference with seasons is that in the depth of snow in January you know that within two months it would be spring...this season for us had no date.

Seeing his pain became very hard and hurt to watch and understanding the simple things like wearing a T-shirt was a huge deal for him to reveal his scars to others. Darren had always lived his life with this and had become accustomed to it however hard it was to look at. On the outside he seemed the "normal" happy-go-lucky guy which he was but you never saw the pain he went through or knew he may constantly have. Every day, he was in some form of pain.

How I Survived 5 Kidney Transplants and Won!

Being brought into that world was shocking to see and upsetting to know, especially since there wasn't really much I could do about it. Nobody ever wished to see somebody they loved dearly, in some form of discomfort, every single day.

Coming home to an empty home three times a week and not knowing how he'd return, sometimes he'd be vomiting with a headache or on odd times he would be fine but just overly tired. I never ever felt that this would be something which would be with us forever or that I would lose him. I always knew that this stage of our life was only for a time but I never knew for how long it would last. I did feel like the unhelpful helper, somebody who was wanting to do everything, when there was nothing I could physically do.

Our honeymoon was beautiful but also sad since, even at a stage where we should've been relaxing and enjoying each other's company, he still had to go and be in some form of pain and was drained because of dialysis.

I remember thinking when Darren explained to me about Lee Ferrigon wanting to be a donor (Lee is Darren's good friend) It was very strange though, at the time, a few close friends were being tested but, to me, Darren never seemed fully at peace with it. Lee continued asking so much that I remembered him doing the testing but it was almost never really spoken of in our home, simply because deep down we thought the results would return "not a match" and that would be the end of that road only for the results to be the total opposite.

It seemed everything was lining up perfectly and within no time a date was set, the end of this chapter seemed nearer but like any good book just before it ended, it was getting a little harder. The hospital trips to Oxford became more often and Darren seemed to be in a different level of pain while they prepared his body for his new kidney.

The day finally came and the feelings were overwhelming. I was so emotional and extremely grateful that this was going to happen. That day changed everything, from freedom to travel to starting a family. The world was now open to us - the weight of "when" had finally been lifted!

Dad

My name is Glen Ferguson, the father of Darren and Pastor of Faith Dimensions Ministries Church, based in Wolverton Milton Keynes. Darren was born on 20th February 1981 at Kettering General Hospital, Kettering, Northamptonshire. He was diagnosed with Chronic Renal Failure which caused a thirty-year struggle of fighting for his life.

My wife Lu and I were told it was unlikely he'd live beyond the age of seven and if he did, would suffer from rickets and have his growth stunted. The predictions were coming to pass since before the age of three our son died three times and each time was revived.

As an infant Darren spent most of his first two years in Great Ormond Street Hospital in London, in fact he was a patient there until he was twelve and then was transferred to the Royal Free Hospital in London. I've seen my son fight for his life and at different times it seemed as if he'd lose the struggle to stay alive.

My faith at times had been stretched to almost breaking point, where I had to make up my mind as to whether I believed and accepted the diagnosis of the renal specialists or I'd continue to hold on and believe that somehow God would come through and do what only He could do. Being that way saved my son's life.

As the years passed and I saw Darren grow from a young baby to a child, he still struggled with his health due to having failing kidneys and it appeared that the older he became, the bigger the problems.

I recalled two torturous nights:

Darren has had five kidney transplants, but I'll never forget two nights in his struggle.

In spite of his many years of pain and health issues, for the most part Darren has been a very jovial and happy child, in fact over the years a lot of sick people have drawn strength and hope from how he has coped and handled his health issues. But I will never forget the look of total despair and hopelessness in his eyes when at the age of fourteen and after yet another operation, the transplanted kidney ruptured in the main vein. This was at The Royal Free Hospital and one of Darren's lowest points to date.

The second and by far the most painful and difficult night in the history of my experience in Darren's kidney story, has to be when he was twenty and by this time had transferred to Churchill Hospital in Oxford.

It was a Wednesday night, a very dark, cold and rainy night, my wife and I received a phone call from the hospital telling us that it was likely our son would die that very night and we should get to the hospital as soon as possible.

We drove at speed from Milton Keynes where we lived to Oxford and upon our arrival, we entered Darren's ward. He was lying on a bed surrounded by five top renal specialists. I ran towards his bed and as I did, he screamed: "Get my dad." I said: "Son I'm here, I'm holding you."

The doctors told me that he was already blind.

One doctor then took a scalpel and prodded him in the base of his foot but he didn't respond. The doctor then told me he was paralysed and his organs were shutting down. This was followed by five major convulsions and my heart and mind went into overdrive.

Seeing what was going on I immediately prayed, asking God to reverse what was being said to me about death closing in, instead affirming that Jesus was the resurrection and since He gave Darren to us, I called on Him to restore my son and He did.

Eventually, we received two remarkable reports:

Due to the many medical issues and drugs Darren had taken all his life, the doctors said he'd not be able to father a child – he is now married with two beautiful daughters.

Darren has had FIVE kidney transplants and is the only person who has had so many transplants and lived. He has defied medical science and is a living, walking miracle!

I'm grateful for all the doctors have done for my son but I know that if it had not been for the grace and healing power of my Lord Jesus Christ, my son would not be alive today, I therefore give God all glory, honour and praise.

The Thoughts Of A Mother

It has been a long and winding road – quite a journey. To see my son, Darren the one that we love and celebrate today is such a far cry from the child that was born on the 20th February 1981. Having lived through Darren's medical condition for so many years, just getting on with it, it is quite hard to articulate one's thoughts but I will try.

We arrived at Kettering General Maternity Unit on the 19th February 1981 for a scheduled caesarean-section, eagerly anticipating the arrival of our second child following a very good and enjoyable pregnancy. He arrived in the afternoon, however, I wasn't able to meet him until the next day due to the surgical procedure.

He was so tiny, thin, weighing 4lbs 2oz... a beautiful baby with long wispy hair - here was our son. After being discharged and now at home, our family was complete. We were happy.

We noticed from very early that Darren slept for hours and I mean for hours – and although we'd frequently check on him I just knew something was wrong. He'd sleep for nearly 8 hours and even when we woke him up he was still lethargic, somewhat limp and not very engaging in breast feeding. I observed him for the next few days, having changed to bottle feeding in the hope that this would be better, yet he continued to sleep for hours. Alarms were now ringing especially after so many hours and his nappy was virtually dry and his skin started to look saggy. Something was wrong with my beautiful son.

An urgent appointment was made to see our doctor. The doctor said: *"Mrs Ferguson your son is chronically dehydrated and we must get him to a hospital immediately."*

I was numb, my heart raced and my mind was going frantic.

I was advised: *"Go home and pack some things for him and we'll arrange for an ambulance to take Darren to Kettering General."*

Leave my baby with strangers? I wept. He was barely 3 weeks old but I stayed with him until the ambulance came. And yet I needed to get home to sort out our elder son and still get to the hospital.

How I Survived 5 Kidney Transplants and Won!

Lee, what was I going to do with him who was only 2½? Think Lu, think!! I went into survival mode, got home and rang my husband at work. I told him the situation and that he needed to come home immediately. I arranged for Lee to stay with a friendly neighbour until my husband arrived to collect him. Nothing could prepare me for what I saw when I arrived at the hospital. They took me to my son who was in a side room and my heart felt like it had stopped! There he was wired to tubes in every orifice of his tiny body. I stood at his crib and cried. My baby...

I heard a voice calling my name: *"Mrs Ferguson, Mrs Ferguson."*

I tried getting myself together and turned to see a doctor and nurse behind me. "Darren's condition is very critical and we're not equipped to provide adequate care for him and he must be transferred to one of the best hospitals - Great Ormond Street in London...." My heart was broken. I felt lost, totally helpless and said a little inward prayer: *'Dear God, please don't let my son die.'*

***

It seemed like an eternity before my husband arrived with our son Lee and

Darren was taken by ambulance all the way to Great Ormond Street Hospital. I accompanied him, my husband and Lee following on. On arrival, a doctor and two nurses were waiting for him, he was immediately rushed to the high dependency critical unit, laid on a bed with a heart monitor attached. Things were frantic for what seemed like forever as I paced the corridors waiting for someone to tell me that my son was going to be alright. I later found out that he was critical and we came very close to losing him. *Why didn't I bring him sooner?*

Vial upon vial of blood was taken from him and there were tubes and wires everywhere as they tried to hydrate him. Finally, I was allowed in the room and this was the beginning of a 30-year journey.

We were told that his urethra valve was blocked and had damaged his kidneys; one was non-functioning and the other had a 25% function, he'd require immediate surgery which he proceeded to have. Whilst in surgery, his heart stopped 3 times, thank God for the monitor that alerted them.

Darren was diagnosed with Chronic Renal Failure and would ultimately need a kidney transplant. I wasn't prepared for that. How were we going to cope? Somehow, we did. We had to.

The joy when he was allowed out of hospital for the first time after being admitted was at Easter. It was a treat, the whole family together again in our home, albeit for one day.

Darren's life journey has taken many twists and turns from there on and it was hard, and painful to relive those moments....

One of the most devastatingly painful memories was when they found a suitable kidney. Devastating? Painful? That should be an ecstatic moment and yes it normally would be....

Darren was prepped for surgery. The kidney had arrived at the hospital and his Dad and I followed him as we always had. *'The procedure will take approximately four hours. He's in good hands'*, were the reassuring words of the Consultants.

Hours later they came out and said, "Everything went extremely well. The kidney is working well and Darren's passing urine. He'll be in recovery then taken back to his room." We wept with relief.

My husband needed to go home to collect our son and bring him to see his brother.

As time passed and Darren was being monitored, I noticed concern on the faces of the attending nurses. The Consultants were called and there was a lot of movement but nothing at this point, was said to me.

***

A machine was bought in (I was familiar with this; it was a scanner) why was this needed? It was just procedure, I told myself. After quite some time I heard: *"Mrs Ferguson, can I see you outside please?"* The Consultant asked. My heart began to race since Darren was coming around.

"I'll be back in a moment," I said, leaning over to kiss my son.

"I'm sorry Mrs Ferguson but Darren's kidney has just ruptured in the main vein and we have to take him back into surgery to remove the kidney immediately."

How I Survived 5 Kidney Transplants and Won!

I screamed, sobbing profusely and called my husband. I said, uncontrollably, *"Glen, please get back here. Darren's kidney has just ruptured and has to be removed."*

I can only imagine what he felt...

My God, how am I going to tell Darren? I asked as I attempted to compose myself and went back into his room. A frail voice said: "Mum did it work? Is my new kidney working?" How do you tell your son no, sorry son? Somehow, I did and the anguish I saw on my son's face at that moment has been etched on my mind. Ten hours after his initial transplant he was back in surgery to remove the now ruptured kidney.

Throughout his life, Darren faced many painful moments, critical infections, near death encounters and just getting to the hospital in the "nick of time" moments in addition to transplants, rejections, false alarms and disappointments coupled with years of dialysis. Seeing it take its toll, we were rendered helpless but knew that somehow, one day the Lord would help us...then Lee Ferrigon, a virtual stranger came into our lives. As a family, we would forever be grateful for the gift this young man gave our son.

Darren Ferguson

The thoughts of a mother...despite the years of pain, anguish and times of simply not knowing how but that God would, today, I'm overwhelmed when I see how that one-time frail, lifeless, chronically sick baby has grown to become a healthy, strong young man, a husband and a father.

I'm so proud of Darren.

Sachel Grant

Having known Darren for over 17 years, I've witnessed just a small part of his journey. Seeing Darren once or twice a week connected to various machines was often heart breaking. I was however in awe of the relationship he had with the staff and the other patients. It was as if it was Darren's Ward. He was always smiling, encouraging and giving others hope, yet, that in itself made me sad. He had been in there for so long and too often which is why they knew him really well.

When I first became friends with Lee (Darren's brother) and visited the family home, I could see how the sickness dictated Darren's life. Everything and anything was around dialysis and all that went with it. He would often smile and be the joker but as I got to know him deeper, I knew he was hurting. He would have some rough days and there were days when I knew the pain was unbearable. Days when I knew he wanted to give up.

During those darkest days it was so hard to see him go through so much pain. Whether it was trips to Milton Keynes or Oxford Hospital, visiting him at his parents' home, later at his brother's and then his own home; was heart wrenching. Someone so young and so nice was going through so much and for so long. But knowing he was a child of the God who'd healed his mother of cancer and healed so many others of their ailments/diseases/sicknesses, I wondered when it would be Darren's turn? A couple of times a week, we used to just sit after I picked him up from dialysis. Sometimes no conversation was necessary but we'd often talk for hours about things which concerned either of us. I definitely believe that was where our relationship grew, in those quiet and times, maybe because he couldn't run away!

It was another close friend of mine, Lee Ferguson, who gave his kidney to Darren six years ago and seeing one friend giving a kidney and the other receiving it was simply mind blowing. I was honoured I was the bait God had used for their friendship and then the donation.

In 2012 I ran the London Marathon and raised nearly £2,000 towards Kidney Research UK and I chose that charity because of Darren and wore a t-shirt with pride because of him. Seeing Darren now simply makes my heart smile and knowing the pain and sacrifice he went through. He has come a long way and is still standing.

Darren, for me, has always been a warrior and everyone knows he was a people person but there were very few people he'd let into his 'inner circle'.

When I see the scars on his body, they are a reminder of the soldier he was and the wars he has been through. God knows how much one can bear and seeing what Darren has borne shows he was one special and amazing man. I, for one, am just so proud of the journey he has undertaken. So proud.

Lee Ferguson

It's hard to even recall the many years watching my brother suffer from renal failure. When I saw what God had done for Darren and how much his life had been transformed I made a conscious effort to remember just how bad things were for him.

When visiting Darren in the hospital and seeing the tubes, the monitors and hearing the reports there were many times I honestly believed I would lose my brother. Often times I would witness him being crippled, in pain, either from surgery or the constant torment of being hooked up to a dialysis machine that would leave him lifeless and often times gave him infections which would put him back in the hospital. Darren was in constant pain.

I remembered when Darren had to have a dialysis line attached to his neck, it was one of the most horrific things I'd ever seen but was in awe of his strength and determination to keep it moving forward regardless of how he felt. He'd jump on his drums and play his little heart out and this often reduced me to tears and I'd always pray God would do something for my brother.

Another vivid key moment in his life was when he was offered a kidney, finding out if it was a perfect match. Joy and excitement mixed with trepidation and questions would come to mind. *"Is this really it?" "What if it fails again?"* All natural responses we had as a family but when we were all by Darren's bedside and he opened his eyes for the first time after coming out from the anesthetic, he quietly whispered, *"Did it work?"*

That moment was so special to us as a family as for the first time ever, we knew this was the moment our son and brother's life would change forever.

It was hard to express how all of this made me feel as Darren's older brother. He was a true warrior and an inspiration to so many people and I knew his life was and would be a testimony to the world of just how good God is.

Charmaine Golley

Darren has been in my life since I was 5 days old. I know this to be true since my Mum had recorded it in my baby book.

My memories of Darren started at a small church in Slough and in our National Conventions where we'd mess about (fondly known as "ramping") to the present day where we are both married with two kids. Through this rollercoaster called "Life", we always kept in contact via daily phone calls or texts to each other.

Darren never really ever talked about his illness with me when we were younger and I guess I lived in oblivion as to how he dealt with it. I remembered the evening he called and told me he'd nearly died after a failed kidney transplant. I don't know if he even remembered making the call but I do - clearly. It was then that I realised that my best friend had life and death moments.

Darren was my hero for different reasons; for never ever complaining about what he'd to live with and for always putting others first, even when he needed someone to put him first. The day I found out he was going to get a transplant after the many prayers and the tears I knew had been shed, was amazing. All our prayers had been answered and if there was ever a doubt about God's existence and his awesome power, all that would've surely been washed away. I visited Darren the same week he got out of hospital and knew that everything would be different for him after that day

After his transplant, Darren went from strength to strength becoming a daddy to two beautiful little girls, one of whom I'm proud to call my Goddaughter. Darren has been there for me like no other friend; getting me through the deaths of two people very close to me within the space of two years; always there at the other end of the phone, giving advice and putting me in my place whenever I needed it.

Darren is my best friend and we don't even call each other by name but by the endearment - "Bestie" - and the day Darren received his transplant was the day God let me keep my best friend.

Bethane Charles – Nurse

Darren Ferguson came to me as a transfer from Paediatric Care at Great Ormond Street Hospital a few weeks after his 17th birthday. It was unusual to take a patient so young in adult care and these days he'd have gone through our 'young adult' service. In 1998 he got me.

Darren was a scared and somewhat resentful young man with a history of a lifetime of dialysis and failed transplantation. Now I'd say he gave me every one of the grey hairs I presently have and I'm sure that is true. He needed to start on dialysis which he was trained to do himself. We had many discussions (at varying heat levels) over whether he carried out his dialysis as trained. He swore he did but his 'numbers' told me otherwise. Sometimes he told me when he missed something –a drug, a dialysis – of course I always knew whether what he said was true or not but he was a teenager with a normal teenage desire to be, well, normal. He had renal failure as a baby and had never had a 'normal' life. His parents watched and I watched, as over the next few years he did what a lot of teenagers do, he rebelled. We despaired. We watched as his health deteriorated and we wondered how to help. There were girlfriends and emotional upsets as he tried to lead a teenager's life with his renal challenges. As his renal Mum I saw them all. But we never managed to fall out despite his failure to listen to me. It became like a parent and child relationship and however hard he pushed I didn't give up, and somehow he got through.

In 2002 Darren had a kidney transplant that worked and this was his chance to get his life back and for a while, all looked good. I hoped I wouldn't be putting Darren on dialysis for a very long time. The transplant lasted until 2005 and then failed. Darren had to return to dialysis with a very poor chance of ever getting another transplant due to the number of transplants he previously had, plus infections and blood transfusions. Although he was older, his outlook was bleaker than ever. He was still in his early 20's and facing a lifetime of dialysis. He had some unpleasant complications, painful bone problems and a network of scars. We'd one ray of sunshine when he married Amanda but he knew and I knew, that his life was going to be one long struggle. His only option was haemodialysis, a regime involving three evenings a week spent in the renal unit having dialysis. Darren was working full time, trying to make a marriage work and spending what must've felt like half his life in the dialysis unit.

A lot of the time he did what he was asked. A lot of the time he didn't. Darren would turn up late for dialysis regularly making it impossible to carry out a proper treatment. He needed to be on treatment for 4½ hours each time but he'd arrive an hour later than he should and complete only 3½ hours on the machine. His blood tests were dreadful and his bones continued to deteriorate. He wouldn't take his tablets and ignored his dietary advice but Darren had such a charming way that often staff almost believed him. It was endlessly frustrating to deal with him. As a health care worker I knew I had to try to get through to him since I did not want to see him suffering an early painful death. Sometimes I'd want to shout at him, shake him, do something to get through to him to get him to work with us and not against us. We'd have so many discussions and arguments. There were tantrums, sometimes tears but all he'd do was enough to stay alive but not enough to stay well.

In 2011 the seemingly impossible happened.

After six years a donor came forward. Many people had been tested for Darren but were never a match due to his blood type and we did not expect a match to ever be found. This donor was not related but the match was good enough to make transplant a possibility after a complex treatment to lower the amount of antibodies in Darren's blood. Even then, he had to accept that the transplant might not work. His doctor set all the risks out in a letter to him and he decided to take his last chance for a normal life. The transplant went ahead, and it worked.

A couple of years later, I got the call I never expected. Darren was going to be a daddy. Imani was born beautiful and healthy and Brianna swiftly followed. After all Darren had gone through in his life, he now was a family man. I've watched over the last two decades as Darren has grown up and there are not many jobs where you have this level of involvement in another's life over so many years. Darren has made me angry many, many times, made me frustrated, made me want to shake some sense into him. He has also made me laugh so many times. And I admit, he made me cry when he said he was going to be a father.

Darren continues to face uncertainties in his life, although it's hoped his transplant will last forever, the odds are against it and there'll be new challenges to face. Though I'm not getting any younger, I expect to be here for him for some time.

KIDNEY DISEASE IS A SILENT KILLER:
Learn About This Deadly Disease

What Are The Kidneys?

The kidneys play key roles in body function, not only by filtering the blood and getting rid of waste products, but also by balancing the electrolyte levels in the body, controlling blood pressure, and stimulating the production of red blood cells.

The kidneys are located in the abdomen toward the back, normally one on each side of the spine. They get their blood supply through the renal arteries directly from the aorta and send blood back to the heart via the renal veins to the vena cava. The kidneys have the ability to monitor the amount of body fluid, the concentrations of sodium and potassium, and the acid-base balance of the body. They filter waste products of body metabolism.

- Symptoms of kidney failure are due to the build-up of waste products and excess fluid in the body that may cause weakness, shortness of breath, lethargy, swelling, and confusion. Inability to remove potassium from the bloodstream may lead to abnormal heart rhythms and sudden death. Initially kidney failure may cause no symptoms.

- There are numerous causes of kidney failure, and treatment of the underlying disease may be the first step in correcting the kidney abnormality.

- Some causes of kidney failure are treatable and the kidney function may return to normal. Unfortunately, kidney failure may be progressive in other situations and may be irreversible.

- The diagnosis of kidney failure usually is made by blood tests measuring creatinine, and glomerular filtration rate.

- Treatment of the underlying cause of kidney failure may return kidney function to normal. Lifelong efforts to control blood pressure and diabetes may be the best way to prevent Chronic kidney disease and its progression to kidney failure . As we age kidney function gradually decreases.

- If the kidneys fail completely, the only treatment options available may be dialysis or transplant.

Many people right now are not even aware they have the condition and are suffering. This is because there are few or no symptoms until the disease is quite advanced and can often come as a major shock to those who are first diagnosed because for a long period they feel fine and then out of the blue they start to feel unwell or get that bad news just from a general checkup. Kidney disease affects anyone at any age although certain factors may mean you are a greater risk of developing the illness.

Chronic kidney disease also known as chronic renal disease, is progressive loss in kidney function over a period of months or years. The symptoms of worsening kidney function are not specific, and might include feeling generally unwell and experiencing a reduced appetite.

It's a common condition often associated with getting older. Anyone can get it, although it's more common in black people and people of south Asian origin.

Kidney failure can get gradually worse over time and eventually the kidneys may stop working altogether, but this is uncommon. Many people with kidney disease are able to live long, largely normal lives.

How I Survived 5 Kidney Transplants and Won!

Kidney disease is usually caused by other conditions that put a strain on the kidneys. Often it's the result of a combination of different problems.

Kidney failure can be caused by:

- High blood pressure – over time, this can put strain on the small blood vessels in the kidneys and stop the kidneys working properly

- Diabetes – too much glucose in your blood can damage the tiny filters in the kidneys

- High cholesterol – this can cause a build-up of fatty deposits in the blood vessels supplying your kidneys, which can make it harder for them to work properly

- Kidney infections

- Blockages in the flow of urine – for example, from recurrent kidney stones or an enlarged prostate

Just to name a few, but there are other things that can bring on renal failure.

Kidney failure can be diagnosed using blood and urine tests. These tests are used to look for high levels of certain substances in your blood and urine that are signs your kidneys aren't working properly.

If you're at a high risk of developing kidney disease, for example, you have one of the conditions mentioned above you may be advised to have regular tests to check for CKD so it's picked up at an early stage.

The results of your blood and urine tests can tell you the stage of your kidney disease. This is a number that reflects how severe the damage to your kidneys is, with a higher number indicating more serious kidney failure.

Treatments for Chronic Kidney Disease

In a proportion of people with kidney disease, the condition will eventually get to a point where their kidneys stop working.

This rarely happens suddenly, so there should be time to plan the next stage of your treatment so make sure you get all the correct information before making a decision.

One of the options when Kidney failure reaches this stage is to have dialysis. This is a procedure to remove waste products and excess fluid from the blood. Your body somehow needs to remove the waste so if your kidneys are failing it is only a matter of time before you will have to start treatment.

There are two main types of dialysis:

- Haemodialysis: This involves diverting blood into an external machine, where it's filtered before being returned to the body. Haemodialysis is usually done about three times a week, either at hospital or at home. Peritoneal dialysis is normally done at home several times a day, or overnight.

  - Peritoneal dialysis – this involves pumping dialysis fluid into the space inside your stomach to draw out waste products from the blood passing through vessels lining the inside of your stomach.

If you don't have a kidney transplant, treatment with dialysis will usually need to be lifelong.

Darren Ferguson

Life On Dialysis

Many people on dialysis have a good quality of life. If you're otherwise well, you should be able to continue doing most day to day routines but every case is different.

Most people can remain on dialysis for many years, although the treatment can only partially compensate for the loss of kidney function and having kidneys that don't work properly can place a significant strain on the body.

Sadly, this means that people can die while on dialysis if they don't have a kidney transplant, particularly elderly people and those with other health problems. Dialysis normally suits someone who is younger because it does put a lot of pressure on your body and can become draining. Unfortunately for adults over 75 some may only survive for two to three years because the pressure just becomes too much, not just physically but emotionally. It really can take its toll on anybody no matter what age you are.

It is important to be know that survival rates of people on dialysis have improved over the past decade and are expected to continue improving in the future just because technology, science and medication are always improving which in the long run is helping more people.

Kidney Transplants

An alternative to dialysis for people with severely reduced kidney function is a kidney transplant.

This is often the most effective treatment for advanced kidney disease, but it involves major surgery and taking medication to stop your body from attacking the donor organ for the rest of your life.

You can live with one kidney, which means donor kidneys can come from recently deceased or living donors.

But there's still a shortage of donors, and sometimes you could wait months or years for a transplant.

You may need to have dialysis while you wait for a transplant.

Survival rates for kidney transplants are extremely good nowadays. About 90% of transplants still function after five years and many work usefully after 10 years or more.

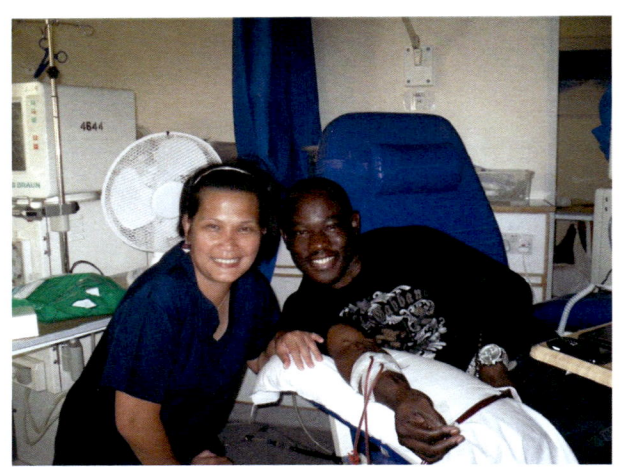

Darren Ferguson

How I Survived 5 Kidney Transplants and Won!

About The Author: Darren Ferguson

Darren James Ferguson, a husband, a father, a son, a brother and so much more, has always had the will to win and has been doing so from a young age, when faced with his most traumatic challenge - Chronic Kidney Failure. At just 7 years of age, when doctors had already given up on him in hospital when his heart had stopped beating - three times - he somehow battled through. And yet, years later, after a long and painful journey, fighting depression and with failing kidney problems, Darren is still here, telling his story.

A very loyal person and member of his local church, Darren finds strength in attending every Sunday and having his loving, loyal and devoted family members and friends around him. And as a father of two, who adores his children, he is always doing his best to protect them from the nightmare that lingers over him each and every day...and it is his faith in God that makes him hold on and believe his journey is finally over.

A family man and drummer who loves music and sports, his wish to be a professional footballer was never attained due to ill health and so he has been unable to achieve that dream; still, that never stopped him from supporting and loving his team, Manchester United fan and still follow tennis and boxing.

Know that Darren has not experienced not 1, not 2, not 3, not 4 but 5 Kidney transplants...let that sink in...FIVE KIDNEY TRANSPLANTS and here he is, alive, telling the tale. Through his sheer determination and a never-say-die attitude, Darren has come face to face with some of his most serious battles – and won.

Though his journey has been painful, there have been many lessons for him to learn, including taking a long look at himself and knowing he always needed to try his best whether as a bubbly person or just give others a reason to smile. Warm-hearted and caring, he invites you to take the journey with him and learn more about this man who should have died at 7 to having the pleasure of meeting the Late Princess Diana.

Darren may get knocked down again but he will get back up and never quit, since with his faith in God as solid as ever, he now stands firm in the knowledge that if God allows the situation to come, he will overcome.

Enjoy this book and Darren's phenomenal journey...*How I Survived 5 Kidney Transplants and Won: the heart moving story of a young man's journey to survive.*

How I Survived 5 Kidney Transplants and Won!